W9-CHI-494

A Note to Parents

DK READERS is a compelling program for beginning readers, designed in conjunction with leading literacy experts, including Dr. Linda Gambrell, Distinguished Professor of Education at Clemson University. Dr. Gambrell has served as President of the National Reading Conference, the College Reading Association, and the International Reading Association.

Beautiful illustrations and superb full-color photographs combine with engaging, easy-to-read stories to offer a fresh approach to each subject in the series. Each DK READER is guaranteed to capture a child's interest while developing his or her reading skills, general knowledge, and love of reading.

The five levels of DK READERS are aimed at different reading abilities, enabling you to choose the books that are exactly right for your child:

Pre-level 1: Learning to read
Level 1: Beginning to read
Level 2: Beginning to read alone
Level 3: Reading alone
Level 4: Proficient readers

The "normal" age at which a child begins to read can be anywhere from three to eight years old. Adult participation through the lower levels is very helpful for providing encouragement, discussing storylines, and sounding out unfamiliar words.

No matter which level you select, you can be sure that you are helping your child learn to read, then read to learn!

DK

LONDON, NEW YORK, MUNICH,
MELBOURNE, AND DELHI

Senior Editor Victoria Taylor
Senior Designer Anna Formanek
Managing Art Editor Ron Stobbart
Publishing Manager Catherine Saunders
Art Director Lisa Lanzarini
Publisher Simon Beecroft
Publishing Director Alex Allan
Pre-production Producer Andy Hilliard
Producer Kara Wallace

For Lucasfilm
Executive Editor Jonathan W. Rinzler
Keeper of the Holocron Leland Chee
Art Director Troy Alders
Director of Publishing Carol Roeder

Reading Consultant
Dr. Linda Gambrell, Ph.D.

First American Edition, 2012
12 13 14 15 16 10 9 8 7 6 5 4 3 2 1
001-186386-Nov/12
Published in the United States by DK Publishing
375 Hudson Street, New York, New York 10014

Page design copyright © 2012 Dorling Kindersley Limited

Copyright © 2012 Lucasfilm Ltd. and ™
All rights reserved. Used under authorization.

All rights reserved under International and Pan-American
Copyright Conventions. No part of this publication may be
reproduced, stored in a retrieval system, or transmitted in any
form or by any means, electronic, mechanical, photocopying,
recording, or otherwise, without the prior written permission
of the copyright owner.
Published in Great Britain by Dorling Kindersley Limited

DK books are available at special discounts when purchased in
bulk for sales promotions, premiums, fund-raising, or
educational use.
For details, contact:
DK Publishing Special Markets
375 Hudson Street
New York, New York 10014
SpecialSales@dk.com

A catalog record for this book is available
from the Library of Congress.

ISBN: 978-0-7566-9810-2 (Paperback)
ISBN: 978-0-7566-9811-9 (Hardcover)

Color reproduction by Alta Image
Printed and bound China by L-Rex Printing Co., Ltd.

Discover more at
www.dk.com
www.starwars.com

Contents

NIAGARA FALLS PUBLIC LIBRARY

DK READERS

READING 3 ALONE

STAR WARS

OBI-WAN KENOBI
JEDI KNIGHT

Written by Catherine Saunders

Legendary Jedi

Meet Obi-Wan Kenobi, a brave Jedi Knight. He went on many missions and fought in many battles to keep the galaxy safe and peaceful.

Obi-Wan Kenobi was born on the planet Stewjon and lived there with his parents and his brother Owen. Young Obi-Wan began to show signs that he had Jedi powers, so he left his family to live on Coruscant. There, Obi-Wan became a youngling and was trained in the ways of the Jedi by Master Yoda.

The best younglings eventually become apprentices, or Padawans, to Jedi Knights. Obi-Wan showed promise, but he was not chosen to be a Padawan.

Padawan training

While many of his friends became Padawans, Obi-Wan Kenobi was sent to work in a mining colony on the Outer Rim of the galaxy. He believed his dream of becoming a Jedi Knight was over, until Jedi Master Qui-Gon Jinn finally spotted his potential. Qui-Gon chose Obi-Wan to be his apprentice and Obi-Wan's life as a Jedi began. As a Padawan, Obi-Wan accompanied Qui-Gon on missions all over the galaxy.

Obi-Wan in his Padawan robes.

The young apprentice learns many things from his powerful Master.

Obi-Wan learned how to use Jedi wisdom, diplomacy, and negotiation to settle disputes, but he also learned how to use his Force powers and combat skills. As the years passed, Obi-Wan's Jedi powers grew stronger and he hoped to be given the chance to face the Jedi Trials. If he passed the Trials, he would finally become a Jedi Knight.

An important mission

A trade dispute gave Obi-Wan the chance to prove himself. The Trade Federation blockaded the planet of Naboo and the galaxy was on the brink of war. Obi-Wan and Qui-Gon helped Queen Amidala of Naboo to escape the blockade. They all set off for Coruscant to seek help.

Qui-Gon and Obi-Wan voyaged through the planet core with Jar Jar Binks on their way to the city of Theed.

Special boy
On Tatooine, the Jedi met
a young boy named Anakin
Skywalker. Qui-Gon could
see that Anakin had the
potential to be a great Jedi.

Unfortunately, the Jedi's ship was damaged by the blockade and they were forced to land on the desert planet of Tatooine for repairs. Here they encountered a mysterious Sith.

Eventually, the Jedi and their passengers made it to Coruscant. The Jedi Council decided that Obi-Wan and Qui-Gon should go back to Naboo and help the Queen defeat the Trade Federation.

On Tatooine, a deadly Sith Lord pursued the Queen of Naboo.

Sith duel

Sith Lord Darth Maul tried to destroy the Jedi on Tatooine. While the Queen and her troops fought the Trade Federation, Obi-Wan Kenobi and Qui-Gon Jinn took on the powerful Sith inside the city's power generator. It was a tough battle. Maul soon separated the Jedi Master from his Padawan and Obi-Wan could only watch as the Sith killed Qui-Gon.

Sith

The Jedi want peace and justice, but the Sith want power. The Jedi believed that they had destroyed their old enemies 1,000 years ago, but they were wrong.

Obi-Wan gained strength and courage from the light side of the Force.

It was time for the young Padawan to prove himself. Although he fought bravely, Maul was able to push Obi-Wan into the generator's core. Luckily, Obi-Wan Kenobi was smarter than Maul. He used the Force to snatch Qui-Gon's lightsaber and jump up and defeat the Sith.

Jedi Knight

The Jedi Council decided that Obi-Wan had proved himself worthy of the title "Jedi Knight" by defeating Maul—he did not need to face the Jedi Trials. Now, as a Jedi Knight, Obi-Wan Kenobi needed an apprentice. Keeping a promise he made to Qui-Gon, Obi-Wan chose Anakin Skywalker as his Padawan.

The apprentice had become the teacher. Obi-Wan tried to teach Anakin how to be a good Jedi.

Master Yoda
Grand Master Yoda was the
wisest and most powerful Jedi.
He sensed that Anakin
Skywalker had much fear
and anger in him and
did not think he should
be trained as a Jedi.

Over the next few years, Obi-Wan
took his young Padawan on many
missions and tried to teach him the
ways of the Force. The Jedi
and Padawan developed a
close friendship. At times,
Obi-Wan wished Anakin
would be more cautious,
but he believed
Anakin was destined
to become a great
Jedi in the future.

Dangerous mission

Obi-Wan and Anakin were given the job of protecting their old friend, Padmé Amidala. The former Queen of Naboo was now a senator in the Galactic Republic, but someone was trying to kill her. When an assassin made an attempt on Padmé's life, the Jedi leapt into action to save her.

Obi-Wan and Anakin were determined to find out who wanted to kill senator Amidala.

Forbidden love

Anakin Skywalker was in love with Padmé, but Jedi are not supposed to form emotional attachments. Padmé felt the same about Anakin so they hid their feelings from Obi-Wan.

Using their piloting and tracking skills, Obi-Wan and his Padawan chased the assassin, Zam Wesell, but she was killed by a poisonous dart before they could find out who she was working for. Obi-Wan examined the poisonous dart for clues.
He ordered Anakin to stay and protect Padmé, while he went off in search of more information.

Clever Jedi

Obi-Wan was determined to find out who wanted to kill Senator Amidala. He learned that the dart came from the planet of Kamino, an aquatic planet located beyond the Outer Rim of the galaxy. When Obi-Wan visited the planet, he received a warm welcome from the Kaminoans. However, he was shocked to learn that they were building a huge clone army, apparently on the orders of deceased Jedi Master, Sifo-Dyas.

Clones
Each clone soldier was genetically identical which means they looked the same. They were bred to follow orders.

Obi-Wan also met Jango Fett, a Mandalorian bounty hunter whose genetic code had been used to make all the clones. The Jedi Council ordered Obi-Wan to bring Jango Fett to Coruscant for questioning. But, the bounty hunter was not prepared to come voluntarily....

Bounty hunter duel

Boba Fett

Jango Fett and his son Boba tried to flee, but Obi-Wan caught up with them before they could board their ship, *Slave I*. The Jedi and the bounty hunter fought a fierce duel. To make matters worse for Obi-Wan, young Boba started firing at him from *Slave I*. Finally, the Jedi realized this was one battle he could not win.

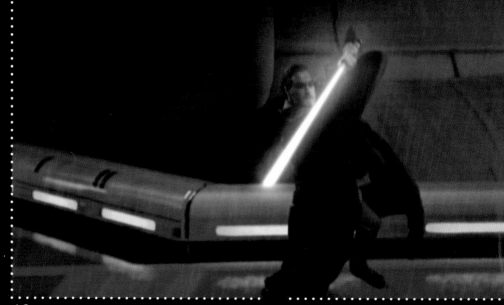

The bounty hunter escaped, but the wise Jedi attached a tracking device to Fett's ship. Obi-Wan followed the bounty hunter to a planet named Geonosis, but even more trouble awaited him there....

An enemy revealed

Obi-Wan was close to uncovering something very big. On Geonosis, he learned that a group of Separatists was plotting to break away from the Republic. They were led by the former Jedi, Count Dooku. Obi-Wan discovered that Dooku had been behind the attempts to kill Padmé and that Dooku and his allies were building a massive droid army. Obi-Wan told the Jedi Council what he had found out before he was captured by Dooku.

Count Dooku
Count Dooku had turned to the dark side and become a Sith Lord. His Sith name was Darth Tyranus.

Dooku tried to convince Obi-Wan to join his army, but the Jedi was not tempted by power. Anakin and Padmé arrived on Geonosis to help Obi-Wan, but they were captured too. Obi-Wan, Anakin, and Padmé were sentenced to death and led to a huge arena to await their fate.

Dooku told Obi-Wan that the Senate was secretly being controlled by a Sith Lord, but Obi-Wan did not believe him.

The Battle of Geonosis

Obi-Wan, Anakin, and Padmé discovered their executioners were three huge creatures—a nexu, a reek, and an acklay. The Jedi and the Senator fought off the beasts, but Dooku sent in droidekas to kill them. Just when it seemed that all was lost, 200 Jedi fighters joined the battle.

Unfortunately, Dooku had been expecting the Jedi and deployed his droid army. The Jedi Knights were outnumbered, until Master Yoda arrived with the huge clone army. The Battle of Geonosis had begun! Dooku used the opportunity to escape, but Obi-Wan was not about to let the Sith go....

In the arena battle on Geonosis, the Jedi were aided by Master Mace Windu.

Jedi duel

Obi-Wan and
Anakin caught up with
Dooku, and prepared
to do battle with him.

Dooku used deadly Force lightning on Anakin.

Obi-Wan wanted them to
attack him together, but
Anakin rushed ahead. Dooku quickly
wounded the impulsive Padawan,
leaving Obi-Wan to duel him alone.

Obi-Wan struggled against Dooku's dark side powers.

Faced with the choice of defeating the Sith or saving the Jedi, Master Yoda was forced to let Dooku escape.

The Jedi fought bravely, but Dooku soon had him at his mercy. He was about to deliver a fatal blow, when Anakin regained consciousness and saved his Master.

Obi-Wan had taught his apprentice well, but the Sith was too strong for him and severed Anakin's hand. Once again, only the timely arrival of Yoda saved the two Jedi.

The Clone Wars

The events on Geonosis were the start of the Clone Wars. The clone army, now called the Grand Army of the Republic, fought many battles against the Separatist Droid Army. During that time the Jedi became generals, rather than peacekeepers. Obi-Wan Kenobi became a great leader, and fought many battles alongside his apprentice Anakin.

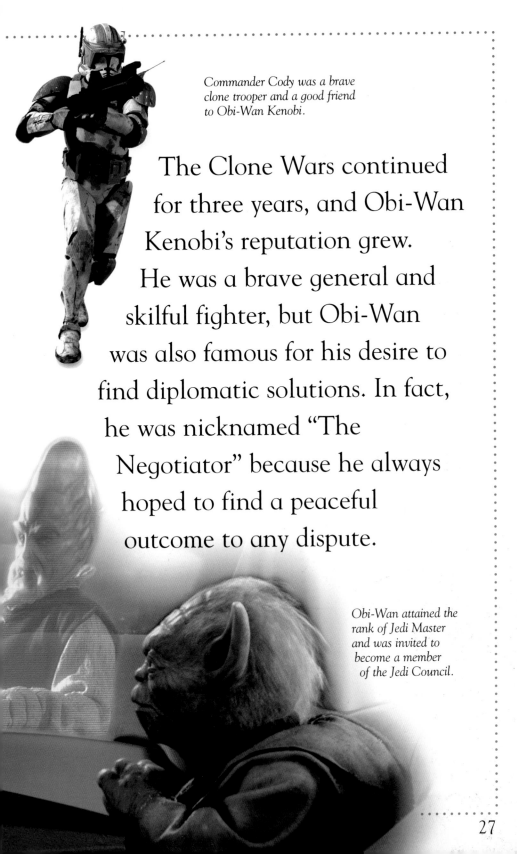

Commander Cody was a brave clone trooper and a good friend to Obi-Wan Kenobi.

The Clone Wars continued for three years, and Obi-Wan Kenobi's reputation grew. He was a brave general and skilful fighter, but Obi-Wan was also famous for his desire to find diplomatic solutions. In fact, he was nicknamed "The Negotiator" because he always hoped to find a peaceful outcome to any dispute.

Obi-Wan attained the rank of Jedi Master and was invited to become a member of the Jedi Council.

The Battle of Coruscant

Obi-Wan and Anakin were sent on a mission to rescue Chancellor Palpatine, who had been kidnapped by Dooku and Separatist leader General Grievous.

For a second time, the Jedi faced Count Dooku in a duel. However, this time the Sith overpowered Obi-Wan using a Force choke. Anakin had to fight Dooku alone.

Encouraged by
Palpatine, Anakin
murdered a
defenseless Dooku—
a violation of the Jedi
Code. Palpatine also

*Dooku was betrayed by
Chancellor Palpatine.*

wanted Anakin to leave Obi-Wan
to die, but the Jedi refused. When
Obi-Wan regained consciousness,
he sensed that he had missed
something important.

With R2-D2's help, Anakin crash-landed the Invisible Hand *after it split in two.*

Jedi wisdom

Obi-Wan was growing deeply suspicious of Chancellor Palpatine. He saw that he was becoming very powerful and Obi-Wan did not trust him. Obi-Wan was also concerned for his former Padwan, Anakin. Obi-Wan tried to talk to him, but the troubled Jedi would not listen.

Obi-Wan was worried that Anakin was more influenced by the politician than the Jedi Council.

Unfortunately, Obi-Wan was called away on a mission to find General Grievous. Without Obi-Wan around to guide him, Anakin listened more and more to Palpatine. Finally, Palpatine revealed his secret identity to Anakin. He offered the Jedi great power and urged him to turn to the dark side. Anakin agreed, taking on a secret Sith identity—Darth Vader.

Obi-Wan felt deeply troubled.

Chancellor Palpatine
Palpatine was the leader of the Senate but he had a secret—he was really a Sith Lord, Darth Sidious. And he was plotting to take over the galaxy.

Cyborg duel

General Grievous was a powerful Separatist leader. Obi-Wan tracked him to the planet of Utapau and faced him in a duel. The Jedi had only one lightsaber, but the General wielded four. Obi-Wan sliced off two of the cyborg's hands to even the odds.

Eventually the Jedi Master killed Grievous by shooting him with the cyborg's own blaster. With Grievous dead, Obi-Wan's mission on Utapau was complete and the Clone Wars were finally over. However, back on Coruscant things were about to get very bad indeed....

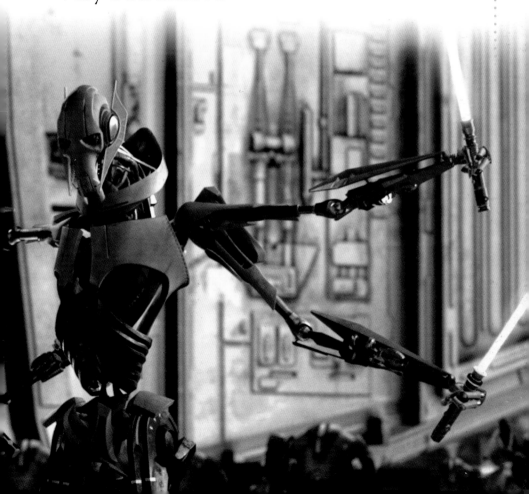

The Jedi purge

While Obi-Wan was on Utapau, Chancellor Palpatine issued Order 66 and the Clone Army turned against the Jedi. Obi-Wan survived an attack by his clone troopers, but when he returned to Coruscant he learned that the Sith Darth Vader had killed all the Jedi in the Jedi Temple.

Obi-Wan realized that things were worse than he ever imagined— Palpatine was a Sith Lord and Vader was his former Padawan, Anakin. Obi-Wan had no choice— he would have to fight his best friend.

Few Jedi survived Order 66.

Epic duel

Obi-Wan tracked his former friend to the planet Mustafar. Full of anger, Vader attacked Obi-Wan. The Jedi Master was a legendary fighter, but so was Anakin, and now he had the power of the dark side of the Force.

This was one of the greatest duels in the history of the galaxy, and one of the most important.

A new enemy
Darth Vader did not
die. Palpatine rescued
him and had him
re-built, using black
armor to protect his
body and a helmet
to help him breathe.

The former friends fought hard,
each determined to win. However,
Anakin had grown arrogant and it
proved to be his downfall. As the
Sith made a daring leap at Obi-Wan,
the Jedi Master was able to strike him
with his lightsaber. Obi-Wan finally
had Anakin at his mercy. But the
Jedi Master was unwilling to kill a
defenseless man. Instead, Obi-Wan
chose to let the Force decide Darth
Vader's fate.

Into hiding

With the galaxy in turmoil and
the Jedi in danger, Obi-Wan turned
his attention to Anakin's wife,
Padmé. The Senator was pregnant,
so Obi-Wan took her to a safe place
to give birth. Obi-Wan knew that
her children would be in danger if
Palpatine learned of their existence,
so he came up with a plan.

*Padmé gave birth to twins—a boy and a girl. But she had no
desire to live without Anakin.*

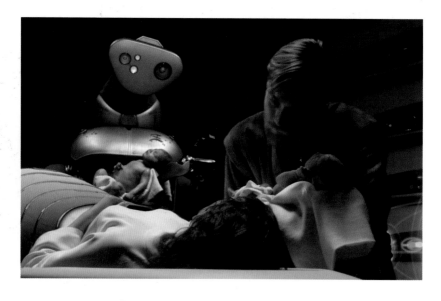

Anakin's stepbrother, Owen, and his wife, Beru, raised Luke Skywalker on Tatooine.

He gave the girl, Leia, to Senator Organa from the planet Alderaan and she was raised as a princess. Obi-Wan took the boy, Luke, to Tatooine. Once he was sure that Anakin's children were safe, Obi-Wan Kenobi went into hiding.

With Palpatine now controlling the galaxy, it was no longer safe to be a Jedi.

Ben Kenobi

Obi-Wan remained on Tatooine where he could check on Luke from a distance. He called himself "Ben" Kenobi and lived a quiet life, keeping his Jedi powers a secret. During that time, the evil Sith Lord Sidious built a powerful Empire. He ruled the galaxy with Darth Vader. Everyone lived in fear of the Emperor, only the Rebel Alliance dared to oppose him.

Obi-Wan decided that the time was right to give Luke his father's lightsaber.

Obi-Wan also offered to begin teaching Luke in the ways of the Force.

One day, Luke was attacked by a Tusken Raider while searching for his new droid, R2-D2. Obi-Wan rescued Luke and immediately saw his Jedi potential. He invited Luke to go on a mission, but he refused. Eventually, Luke changed his mind. It was time for Obi-Wan to become a Jedi once more.

R2-D2

R2-D2 had a message from the Rebel leader, Princess Leia, for Obi-Wan. He had the plans for the Emperor's Death Star and Leia wanted Obi-Wan to deliver them to her father on Alderaan.

Important mission

Obi-Wan needed to deliver Princess Leia's message. He hired a smuggler named Han Solo, his Wookiee co-pilot, Chewbacca, and their ship the *Millennium Falcon*.

Before they could reach Alderaan, it was destroyed by the Death Star.

C-3PO and R2-D2 played holochess against Chewbacca on the Millennium Falcon. Han advised them to let the Wookiee win.

Worse still, the
*Millennium
Falcon* was also
captured by the

The *Millennium Falcon*.

Death Star. As Obi-Wan tried
to disable the Death Star's tractor
beam so the *Millennium Falcon*
could escape, he met his old friend
Darth Vader.

Final duel

Obi-Wan was not surprised to see Vader. In fact, he had been expecting him. Obi-Wan knew exactly what he needed to do to help Luke, Leia, and Han escape. He ignited his lightsaber and prepared to duel.

Vader was happy to duel his former Master, but this time he was determined to win. As the wise old Jedi and the terrifying Sith fought, Vader mocked Obi-Wan. However, as soon as Obi-Wan knew that Luke, Han and Leia were safe, he extinguished his lightsaber and summoned the Force. Seconds before Vader would have struck a fatal blow, Obi-Wan disappeared. The Jedi had left his physical body behind but he would live on as part of the Force.

Guiding light

Being a part of the Force meant Obi-Wan could still guide Luke Skywalker. During the Battle of Yavin, Luke was faced with the task of destroying the Death Star. When the young Jedi hesitated, Obi-Wan advised him to "use the Force."

Luke fired the shot that destroyed the Death Star.

When Luke learned that his father was Darth Vader, Obi-Wan helped him to control his emotions and revealed that he also had a twin sister—Leia.

Only the greatest Jedi such as Anakin Skywalker, Yoda, and Obi-Wan Kenobi have the power to become a part of the living Force.

Later, he told Luke to seek out Yoda in the Dagobah system and persuaded the old Jedi to train him.

Obi-Wan Kenobi was one of the greatest Jedi who ever lived. He went on many missions and fought in many battles to keep the galaxy safe. Now he is one with the Force, joined by Yoda and Anakin as they watch over future generations.

Glossary

Apprentice
A person who is learning a skill.

Aquatic
Related to water. Watery.

Arrogant
Acting superior to others. Having an overly high opinion of oneself.

Assassin
Someone who is hired to kill somebody.

Blockade
Sealing off a place to prevent people entering or leaving.

Bounty hunter
Someone who searches for and captures people for a reward.

Coruscant
One of the most important planets in the galaxy.

Dark side
The part of the Force associated with fear and hatred.

Diplomacy
Sensitivity and tact in dealing with people.

Dispute
An argument or disagreement.

Droid
A kind of robot.

Executioners
An official person who carries out a death sentence.

Force
The energy created by all living things.

Galaxy
A group of millions of stars and planets.

Impulsive
Doing something without thinking about it first.

Jedi Knight
A warrior with special powers who defends the good of the galaxy. Anakin Skywalker, Luke Skywalker and Obi-Wan Kenobi are all Jedi Knights.

Jedi Council
An organized group of Jedi and Jedi Masters who govern the Jedi academies, temples, and other organizations.

Kaminoans
The tall, thin species that lives on the planet Kamino.

Legendary
Famous or well-known for something.

Lightsaber
A Jedi's and Sith's weapon. It has a sword-like blade of pure energy.

Negotiation
Discussing something in order to reach an agreement.

Rebel Alliance
A group of people who want to remove the Emperor from power.

Republic
A nation or group of nations in which the people vote for their leaders.

Separatists
A group of people who want to separate themselves from the Galactic Republic.

Sith
Enemies of the Jedi who use the dark side of the Force.

Suspicious
Unsure whether to trust.

Trade Federation
A group of merchants and transporters who control the movement of goods in the galaxy.

Violation
A crime or act that ignores a rule or agreement.

Youngling
The first stage of Jedi training, before you become a Padawan Learner.